MY COCKAPOO JOURNAL AND NOTEBOOK

LIFE IS BETTER SERIES #35

*A Blank Lined Notebook and Journal
Gift Book for Cockapoo Dog Lovers*

THIS BOOK BELONGS TO

_____

Created by Carrie Wolf

ALL ABOUT COCKAPOOS #1

```
C O C K E R S P A N I E L X E U S W H E A L T H Y
V R X X F U N L O V I N G I R A D A P T A B L E A
E I O E N C Y K S F T G L I O K A V H D Y L L P C
E A R S Y O T U B W O U N O A C O Y E J T A Y D T
J K S L S N K Y F D G B V G N L N R A X Z D E G R
R K R Y E B L Q R J Y E N S U G U Q L B R Q P R A
P U A I G D R E X L G I K F O T L J Q U Z J J O I
C E T F N O N E D I D W Y O A C E I T E T I E O N
O A R E F G I N E D O A A N H U I S F A G Y V M A
P B I S I E E N E D L R T W Y J W A R E K S D I B
P R E S O I C H G P K E P U P O J T B I S T U N L
F G E D R N S T P K E W H L O R U A U L C P O G E
J D W F I W A X I W Y A F P A E N V P T E Y A G B
M B D C O E U B S O Q I A V L N V G D O R C R N P
W I U L A N Z L S N K O D L S C O M P A N I O N
K T A S L D N T V E C A O U E T H F S B B F M J N
Y W N L C H D O J O E O T Y R U R C G E T G K W J
V V J T X T Y L C Q P C D E G B C H P G E N T L E
S M A L L W K B Y Q G D C R E B O Y V X O K K C W
Q P X L S S M A R T R Q B H N O I A N A G K D R U
D D V B Q C O S W I C C B I R V L O V E A B L E
Z E X E R C I S E M D S Q F C N L T V B Z I T I L
```

Cockapoo	Cocker Spaniel	Poodle	hybrid	crossbreed	playful
friendly	low shedding	sturdy	hypoallergenic	small	healthy
smart	cuddly	affectionate	fun loving	grooming	companion
kid friendly	adaptable	curly	wavy	gentle	personable
patient	sweet natured	sociable	trainable	easygoing	stubborn
exercise	obedient	designer dog	long lifespan	loveable	

ALL ABOUT COCKAPOOS #1

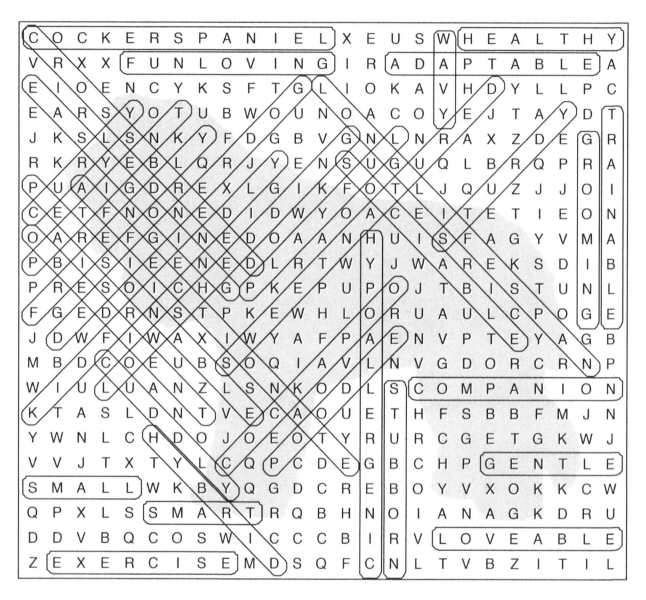

Cockapoo	Cocker Spaniel	Poodle	hybrid	crossbreed	playful
friendly	low shedding	sturdy	hypoallergenic	small	healthy
smart	cuddly	affectionate	fun loving	grooming	companion
kid friendly	adaptable	curly	wavy	gentle	personable
patient	sweet natured	sociable	trainable	easygoing	stubborn
exercise	obedient	designer dog	long lifespan	loveable	

ALL ABOUT COCKAPOOS #1

```
P H U Q P Q V I E X E R C I S E Z H E A L T H Y I
F A F U N L O V I N G I K O S C T Y Y E K E Z S
R R T R F A P G V Y R Y O J M V Q X E R U X P R Z
W C I I V Y P X N A W P I A F F E C T I O N A T E
W U X E E E Q L A D A P T A B L E O N G E W C Z G
O Z P E N N G O A K C Q S R W Y U O I L X I C I N
S O E Y F D T V C Y G D B N D C I W B G N G Y Z M
T B R F W C L O W S F U C R C N K A W E S L H X R
U E S B A D C Y E L X U U O A T E R G A D W B I G
B D O Q V E R C R F O T L P C V H R V D V E M N S
B I N L E C O S S M S N M B O K E Y U C N Y I P O
O E A D A U S B M Y G O G L G L E C B O J D O I C
R N B E S R S L S A C R W L L V Y R D R D K V S I
N T L S Y L B K M G R K O A I B J X S E I Z K J A
X M E I G Y R Z A Y B T O O M F L Y H P I D E C B
J R H G O S E O L N P P F Y M J E S Z E A A G J L
R K G N I N E T L Q Y R E W H I W S E G M N F S E
R P S E N J D K X H O F D H I O N I P R O Y I Y F
J X N R G K I D F R I E N D L Y H G R A P L Z E M
P O O D L E S W E E T N A T U R E D S E N W Z F L
Z H J O D F T R A I N A B L E K C N P C M K J O K
I L W G E W Y V G E N T L E H D M B P F Y L D Q V
```

Cockapoo	Cocker Spaniel	Poodle	hybrid	crossbreed	playful
friendly	low shedding	sturdy	hypoallergenic	small	healthy
smart	cuddly	affectionate	fun loving	grooming	companion
kid friendly	adaptable	curly	wavy	gentle	personable
patient	sweet natured	sociable	trainable	easygoing	stubborn
exercise	obedient	designer dog	long lifespan	loveable	

ALL ABOUT COCKAPOOS #1

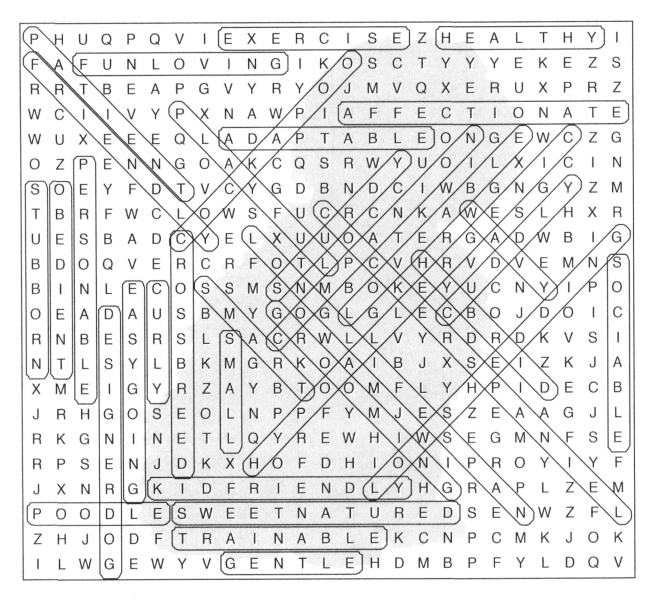

P	H	U	Q	P	Q	V	I	E	X	E	R	C	I	S	E	Z	H	E	A	L	T	H	Y	I
F	A	F	U	N	L	O	V	I	N	G	I	K	O	S	C	T	Y	Y	Y	E	K	E	Z	S
R	R	T	B	E	A	P	G	V	Y	R	Y	O	J	M	V	Q	X	E	R	U	X	P	R	Z
W	C	I	I	V	Y	P	X	N	A	W	P	I	A	F	F	E	C	T	I	O	N	A	T	E
W	U	X	E	E	E	Q	L	A	D	A	P	T	A	B	L	E	O	N	G	E	W	C	Z	G
O	Z	P	E	N	N	G	O	A	K	C	Q	S	R	W	Y	U	O	I	L	X	I	C	I	N
S	O	E	Y	F	D	T	V	C	Y	G	D	B	N	D	C	I	W	B	G	N	G	Y	Z	M
T	B	R	F	W	C	L	O	W	S	F	U	C	R	C	N	K	A	W	E	S	L	H	X	R
U	E	S	B	A	D	C	Y	E	L	X	U	U	O	A	T	E	R	G	A	D	W	B	I	G
B	D	O	Q	V	E	R	C	R	F	O	T	L	P	C	V	H	R	V	D	V	E	M	N	S
B	I	N	L	E	C	O	S	S	M	S	N	M	B	O	K	E	Y	U	C	N	Y	I	P	O
O	E	A	D	A	U	S	B	M	Y	G	O	G	L	G	L	E	C	B	O	J	D	O	I	C
R	N	B	E	S	R	S	L	S	A	C	R	W	L	L	V	Y	R	D	R	D	K	V	S	I
N	T	L	S	Y	L	B	K	M	G	R	K	O	A	I	B	J	X	S	E	I	Z	K	J	A
X	M	E	I	G	Y	R	Z	A	Y	B	T	O	O	M	F	L	Y	H	P	I	D	E	C	B
J	R	H	G	O	S	E	O	L	N	P	P	F	Y	M	J	E	S	Z	E	A	A	G	J	L
R	K	G	N	I	N	E	T	L	Q	Y	R	E	W	H	I	W	S	E	G	M	N	F	S	E
R	P	S	E	N	J	D	K	X	H	O	F	D	H	I	O	N	I	P	R	O	Y	I	Y	F
J	X	N	R	G	K	I	D	F	R	I	E	N	D	L	Y	H	G	R	A	P	L	Z	E	M
P	O	O	D	L	E	S	W	E	E	T	N	A	T	U	R	E	D	S	E	N	W	Z	F	L
Z	H	J	O	D	F	T	R	A	I	N	A	B	L	E	K	C	N	P	C	M	K	J	O	K
I	L	W	G	E	W	Y	V	G	E	N	T	L	E	H	D	M	B	P	F	Y	L	D	Q	V

Cockapoo	Cocker Spaniel	Poodle	hybrid	crossbreed	playful
friendly	low shedding	sturdy	hypoallergenic	small	healthy
smart	cuddly	affectionate	fun loving	grooming	companion
kid friendly	adaptable	curly	wavy	gentle	personable
patient	sweet natured	sociable	trainable	easygoing	stubborn
exercise	obedient	designer dog	long lifespan	loveable	

CONNECT THE DOTS

Taking turns, draw a line horizontally or vertically between two adjacent dots anywhere on the page. The player who completes the fourth side of a square claims the square and puts their initial inside it and takes another turn. Each time a box is completed, the player takes another turn. The game ends when all dots have been connected. The is the player with the most squares.

CONNECT THE DOTS

Taking turns, draw a line horizontally or vertically between two adjacent dots anywhere on the page. The player who completes the fourth side of a square claims the square and puts their initial inside it and takes another turn. Each time a box is completed, the player takes another turn. The game ends when all dots have been connected. The is the player with the most squares.

Taking turns, draw a line horizontally or vertically between two adjacent dots anywhere on the page. The player who completes the fourth side of a square claims the square and puts their initial inside it and takes another turn. Each time a box is completed, the player takes another turn. The game ends when all dots have been connected. The is the player with the most squares.

CONNECT THE DOTS

Taking turns, draw a line horizontally or vertically between two adjacent dots anywhere on the page. The player who completes the fourth side of a square claims the square and puts their initial inside it and takes another turn. Each time a box is completed, the player takes another turn. The game ends when all dots have been connected. The is the player with the most squares.

CONNECT THE DOTS

Taking turns, draw a line horizontally or vertically between two adjacent dots anywhere on the page. The player who completes the fourth side of a square claims the square and puts their initial inside it and takes another turn. Each time a box is completed, the player takes another turn. The game ends when all dots have been connected. The is the player with the most squares.

CONNECT THE DOTS

Taking turns, draw a line horizontally or vertically between two adjacent dots anywhere on the page. The player who completes the fourth side of a square claims the square and puts their initial inside it and takes another turn. Each time a box is completed, the player takes another turn. The game ends when all dots have been connected. The is the player with the most squares.

CONNECT THE DOTS

Taking turns, draw a line horizontally or vertically between two adjacent dots anywhere on the page. The player who completes the fourth side of a square claims the square and puts their initial inside it and takes another turn. Each time a box is completed, the player takes another turn. The game ends when all dots have been connected. The is the player with the most squares.

CONNECT THE DOTS

Taking turns, draw a line horizontally or vertically between two adjacent dots anywhere on the page. The player who completes the fourth side of a square claims the square and puts their initial inside it and takes another turn. Each time a box is completed, the player takes another turn. The game ends when all dots have been connected. The is the player with the most squares.

CONNECT THE DOTS

Taking turns, draw a line horizontally or vertically between two adjacent dots anywhere on the page. The player who completes the fourth side of a square claims the square and puts their initial inside it and takes another turn. Each time a box is completed, the player takes another turn. The game ends when all dots have been connected. The is the player with the most squares.

CONNECT THE DOTS

Taking turns, draw a line horizontally or vertically between two adjacent dots anywhere on the page. The player who completes the fourth side of a square claims the square and puts their initial inside it and takes another turn. Each time a box is completed, the player takes another turn. The game ends when all dots have been connected. The is the player with the most squares.

CONNECT THE DOTS

Made in the USA
Middletown, DE
21 May 2022